CHAPTER ONE

BRINGING DOWN THE POWER OF GOD

Pray like this: Oh thou that troubleth the Israel of my destiny, the God of Elijah shall trouble you today, in the name of Jesus.

Psalms 62:11 says:

God hath spoken once; twice have I heard this; that power belongeth unto God

Note the phrase, "power belongeth unto God."

We have heard with our ears, O God, our fathers have told us, what work thou didst in their days, in the times of old. How thou didst drive out the heathen with thy hand, and plantedst them; how thou didst afflict the people, and cast them out. For they got not the land in possession by their own sword, neither did their own arm save them: but thy right hand, and thine arm, and the light of thy countenance, because thou hadst a favour unto them. Psalms 44:1-3.

A HEARTY CRY

There is a lamentation going on within me for years.

BRINGING DOWN

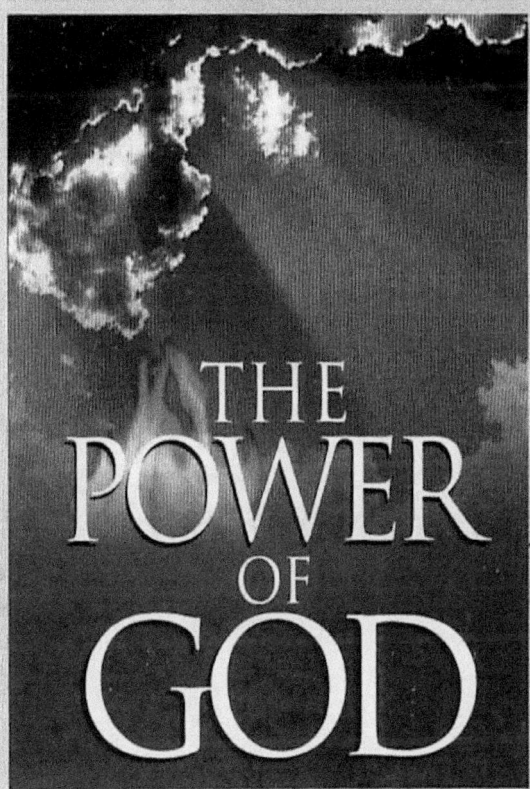

THE
POWER
OF
GOD

DR. D. K. OLUKOYA

Bringing Down The Power Of God

DR. D. K. OLUKOYA

(6) Dr. D. K. OLUKOYA

There is a hearty cry within me day and night that this generation of ours may not witness a true revival before we pass away. This is making me worried and agitated. It would be a disgrace that people like you pass through life without leaving behind an indelible mark. It would be a tragedy to die without making any impact on this generation.

This generation has never witnessed a revival.

During revival in Nigeria at the time of the great Apostle Ayo Joseph Babalola, there was great outbreak of God's power. Many men and women pressed upon him to be healed. People were so many that he could not reach everyone and his voice could not be heard by the teeming multitude of people.

Apostle Ayo then prayed on a particular river and asked the diseased and the impotent to go there for healing. People who drank the water got healed. Those who bathed in it received instant miracles.

So much was the demand for water from the river that it got dried. People lay on the wet mud of the river bed and got healed. This was a raw demonstration of God's power and anointing.

The crusade grounds were literally healing grounds in those days, so much so that people who got to the crusade grounds received God's miracle of healing even without being prayed for.

Our heart's cry should be, "Oh that Thou would rent heavens and wouldest come down that mountain should melt before You." Our heart's cry should be that the Lord should tear up the heavens and come down.

THE NECESSITY OF GOD'S POWER

We need to get back to that time when angels spoke to people face to face, when an average Christian was a generator of God's power. We need to cry to heaven for we cannot continue in the present powerlessness.

What I have found out as I travel all over the world preaching the gospel of Christ, is that almost all the present day Christians are undergoing one form of frustration or the other. There is a kind of restlessness visible on all. This restlessness stems from deep realization that they are falling below God's standard. They are aware that God's power in their lives is not demonstrated as it is supposed to. We need to pray and bring down God's power upon our lives.

It is time for us to kindle and rekindle God's power upon our lives.

If we say that people of the world are demonstrating powerless power, believers should be alive to demonstrate the real power of God. We should be able to show the world the power of God that resides in believers lives.

The tragedy is that many people will not make any head way in their lives if they refuse to bring the power of God down to their situations. If God does not move in their situations then they are completely finished.

Many are so entrenched in the hands of the evil one that unless God's power is invited into their lives they will suffer till death comes.

I once witnessed the confession of a 14-year-old girl who was into witchcraft.

She vomited a padlock whose body looked like a newly born rat. I asked her, "What do you use this padlock for?" She said, "We use it to lock up people." I asked her about how many people she had locked up. She said "Very many, uncountable people." I asked further, "What about your mother?" She said, "I have locked that one up."

Curiously, I further asked, "What has your mother done?" She answered, "She misbehaved and I dealt with her." "Where is that your mother now?" She replied, "She has been on admission in the hospital for 14 months, and the doctors do not know what is happening to her." I then demanded the key to the padlock. She coughed out the small key. I asked her to open the padlock and she did. I then asked her, "Since you have opened this padlock, is your mother now all right?" She responded, "No." According to her, she locked her up with 14 different padlocks. She had just opened one and there remained 13.

Could you see the extent to which the devil could go

in putting people into bondage? That is the more reason we should be filled with the power of God to deal with every contrary situation in our lives.

Many are so entrenched inside the camp of the enemy that unless they bring the power of God down into their lives they would remain in the bondage for life.

Somebody who is 50 years old before he gets converted has used 50 years to accumulate arrows into his life. It would take the power of God for such a person to be freed from such arrows. If the power of God is not brought down into his situation he will suffer until he dies.

My heart weeps for several people who are supposed to be millionaires yet they cannot count money in kobo. My heart cries for those who are supposed to be university lecturers or even professors but they are still struggling to enter into the university.

Without the supernatural working of God coming upon our lives, victory is not possible. This is the

BRINGING DOWN THE POWER OF GOD (11)

reason we must learn how to bring down the power of God into our situations. The apostles realised this deep truth and they prayed: "Oh Lord, stretch forth your hands." Acts 4:23-31 says:

And being let go, they went to their own company, and reported all that the chief priests and elders had said unto them. And when they heard that, they lifted up their voice to God with one accord, and said, Lord, thou art God, which hast made heaven, and earth, and the sea, and all that in them is: Who by the mouth of thy servant David hast said, Why did the heathen rage, and the people imagine vain things? The kings of the earth stood up, and the rulers were gathered together against the Lord, and against his Christ. For of a truth against thy holy child Jesus, whom thou hast anointed, both Herod, and Pontius Pilate, with the Gentiles, and the people of Israel, were gathered together, For to do whatsoever thy hand and thy counsel determined before to be done. And now, Lord, behold their threatenings: and grant unto thy servants, that with all boldness they may speak thy word, By stretching forth thine hand to heal; and that signs and wonders may be done by the name of thy holy child Jesus. And when they had prayed, the place was shaken where they were assembled together; and they were all filled with the Holy Ghost, and they spake the word of God with boldness.

The mother-in-law of a sister who wedded some years ago said to her, "Now you have married my son, you are the second wife and I am the first wife." The wife said, "God forbid!" During the marriage the mother-in-law had presented her with a long loaf of hard bread.

The mother-in-law came again and instructed her to take the bread. The wife could not understand how she started to eat the bread and that was the beginning of her problem. Her menstruation stopped right away and she started to emaciate. However, in one of our meeting days, the power of God descended and the bread she swallowed months ago started to come out of her mouth.

The Lord God Almighty delivered her. We need

such move of God in our lives on daily basis. If the power of God did not come upon her, the problem would have remained in her life.

The Bible says in Ephesians: "We should be strong in the Lord and in the power of His might." We are asked to be strong in the Lord because our enemy is strong in wickedness.

This generation is a funny one. We read and write a lot of history and tell a lot of stories, but we do not seem to be making history.

For us to make history and for our lives to make impact on our generation, we must bring down the power of God into our lives and situations.

It is very unfortunate that there is too much laziness in this generation. Many are too lazy to pray and to read the word of God. This laziness is getting us into serious trouble. Go to the university, you will see lazy students who want to pass without reading. There are lazy men who want to eat without working. There are lazy ministers who want power but they do not want to be disciplined.

It is a tragedy for our generation that nobody has time for God any longer. There is no one who has time to bring down God's power. It is no surprise what the Psalmist lamented in Psalms 74:9 concerning the present-day Christianity.

We see not our signs: there is no more any prophet: neither is there among us any that knoweth how long

It is time for you to challenge and query yourself. Talk to your spirit man. The word of God should be taken seriously and not just as a theory. Get yourself ready.

You are still playing and joking with your Christianity unless you get to the point of holy madness. You are yet to start until you get to the level of madness of the blind Bartimeus. You ought to get to the level of madness of the Syrophonecian woman who after Jesus referred to her as a dog she pleaded for mercy to be shown unto her.

It is time you called God into your personal situation. It is time He came to our lives and make us

His place of abode.

It is true that we have a strong and clever enemy but thank God that through Christ we are stronger and cleverer than he. It is possible for us through God's power to plunder the house of the enemy. It is possible for us to bring the enemy down to where he belongs. Brethren, through Christ we have all it takes to do so.

The enemy has diverted the attention of men so much that they major on minority and the minor on majority.

James 5:17 is challenging. It reads:

Elias was a man subject to like passions as we are, and he prayed earnestly that it might not rain: and it rained not on the earth by the space of three years and six months.

The sentence that is very striking here is "Elias was a man subject to like passions as we are."

The Bible is saying here that Elias was an ordinary man like we are. There was nothing special about him. The Bible is challenging us to be ashamed of ourselves for not being able to perform as Elias.

WHEN THE POWER COMES

We need to pray heaven-tearing prayer. We need to pray the building-shaking prayer. We need to pray such prayer that would bring down the power of God.

When the power of God is brought down upon our lives, idol worshippers would be disgraced and demonic powers would be silenced. There would be great and abundant rain of blessings.

When you bring down the power of God, the stubborn sea confronting you will divide and the dry bones will become a great army. When the power of God is brought down into your situation, there will be supernatural success, there will be strength and miracles would become a daily occurrence for you. Satanic monuments will be removed and all the problems the enemy is throwing at your way will become opportunities. The glory of God will be revealed.

Nothing glamourous will happen until you get to that

level of holy madness. It is not news that a dog bites a man, but when a man bites a dog it becomes a great news. Something might have pushed a man to bite a dog.

When you become desperate then your progress begins. The Lord is waiting for you to get to that state of holy desperation.

We ought to learn about God's hands and how to bring them down. Moving forward would be difficult without the power of God upon your life. The hand of God is synonymous with His power. Miracles, healings and wonders would happen, great expansion and increase would happen and ennoblement and strength would happen, when the power of God is brought down to our situations. The obstacles and oppositions will be melted away and there will be favour and acceptance.

When the power comes down, the obituaries of your enemies will be written. God's arm would give strength and we shall go from crawling to walking, from walking to running and from running to flying.

EFFECTIVE POWER OF GOD

That is why the Bible says that the power of God is great, it is strong, it does great wonders. It is glorious, it is mighty, it is everlasting, it is effectual and sovereign. It is irresistible, incomparable and incomprehensible.

With the power of God all things are possible. With it there is nothing too hard. It can save with many and can save with few. It is the source of all strength and glory.

LEVELS OF MANIFESTATION OF THE POWER OF GOD

There are six levels of manifestation of the power of God. When God's power comes upon a person's life, even enemies would also testify.

1. THE VOICE OF GOD

Psalms 25:3-9: Yea, let none that wait on thee be ashamed: let them be ashamed which transgress without cause. Shew me thy ways, O

Lord; teach me thy paths. Lead me in thy truth, and teach me: for thou art the God of my salvation; on thee do I wait all the day. Remember, O Lord, thy tender mercies and thy lovingkindnesses; for they have been ever of old. Remember not the sins of my youth, nor my transgressions: according to thy mercy remember thou me for thy goodness' sake, O Lord. Good and upright is the Lord: therefore will he teach sinners in the way. The meek will he guide in judgment: and the meek will he teach his way.

When God speaks, creation must obey. When you become the oracle of God and you speak, things would begin to happen. It was God's voice that said, "Let there be light" and there was light. It said to the sea, "Peace be still." Geographers tell us that the sea of Galilee that Jesus spoke peace to is the calmest sea in the world today. From the day Jesus ordered peace on it, the sea has never ceased to obey that voice. What we require most of the time is to hear that voice that says "Peace be still."

2.   THE FINGER OF GOD.

This can be found in Exodus 8: 19:

Then the magicians said unto Pharaoh, This is the finger of God: and Pharaoh's heart was hardened, and he hearkened not unto them; as the Lord had said.

The New Testament reference that is parallel to Exodus 8: 19 is Luke 11:20:

But if I with the finger of God cast out devils, no doubt the kingdom of God is come upon you.

Jesus cast out the devil with the finger of God, which is the least presence of God in a situation. That least presence of God is quite devastating to the kingdom of satan.

3.   THE HAND OF GOD.

This can be found in Psalm 44:2:

How thou didst drive out the heathen with thy hand, and plantedst them; how thou didst afflict the people, and cast them out.

The hand is larger than the finger. When the hands

of God come to a problem, its root would be discovered and solution would be found.

4. THE ARM OF THE LORD.

This level could be located in Psalm 118:15:

The voice of rejoicing and salvation is in the tabernacles of the righteous: the right hand of the Lord doeth valiantly.

The same idea is found in Psalm 89:21:

With whom my hand shall be established: mine arm also shall strengthen him.

When the arm of the Lord comes into your situation, chronic and stubborn problems would be solved.

5. THE OUTSTRETCHED ARM OF GOD.

This level can be found in Exodus 15:12:

"Thou stretchedst out thy right hand, the earth swallowed them."

Thou stretchedst out thy right hand, the earth swallowed them.

The same idea is found in Acts 4:30:

By stretching forth thine hand to heal; and that signs and wonders may be done by the name of thy holy child Jesus.

When the outstretched hand of God comes to your situation, creative miracles would happen. For example, the organs that were absent from the body would be recreated.

6. THE THUNDER OF GOD'S POWER.

This can be found in Job 26: 4:

To whom hast thou uttered words? and whose spirit came from thee?

When the thunder of God's power comes into your situation, your enemies would see you and run away. When the thunder of His power comes into your situation, those who refuse to leave you alone will die, He will fight for you like a mighty terrible one and people may even gather and call you a witch or wizard.

HOW TO BRING DOWN GOD'S POWER INTO YOUR SITUATION

1. Renounce every sin

A sinner cannot bring down the power of holy God, therefore, leave backbiting, gossiping, lying, fornication, drunkenness and other sins.

2. Aggressive praise

Paul and Silas sang aggressively in the prison and God's power came down. They praised God and earthquake of deliverance started to take place. After much prayer and nothing seems to work, turn to praises. Praise God for a long time and aggressively.

3. Targeted, fervent prayers

This kind of prayer can bring down the power of God.

4. Violent faith

I mean faith that does not give room for an alternative route.

5. Wait on God

Waiting on God means your daily devotion to God. Have seasons of waiting on God. Wait on Him if you want to go from strength to strength and from glory to glory.

6. Have thirst and hunger for more of God

If you hunger for God, you would long for knowledge of Him. His word would become your bosom friend.

7. Grow into maturity

Maintain your integrity and have a solid character so that God can dwell in you.

8. Obey God in everything.

You need the power of God to come down to your situation. You need to dismantle every conspiracy against your destiny in prayer. Do not joke with the contrary powers that vowed to see your end. You need to pray the kind of prayer that can tear down heavens. God is still available to show His might on your behalf. He can still surprise you today. He can still shock doctors and other people who think that your situation is irreparable.

God is still in the business of raising the poor out of dunghill and setting him among the princes. He is still in the business of putting laughter on people's faces.

Immediately the Philistines took Samson and tied him up, the Spirit of God and the power of God came on him and the rope which the enemy used to tie him broke to pieces. When the power of God comes upon your life your bondage and shackles will be broken.

PRAYER POINTS

1. Power of God, arise and fight for me, in the name of Jesus.

2. O voice of God, speak solution to my problems, in the name of Jesus.

3. O finger of God, arise and pursue my pursuers, in the name of Jesus.

4. O hand of God, arise and kill my goliath, in the name of Jesus.

5.   O outstretched hand of God, arise and promote me by fire, in the name of Jesus.

CHAPTER TWO

POWER TO SOAR

Raise your right hand and pray thus:

1. Every conspiracy in the heavenlies against my destiny, scatter by fire, in the name of Jesus.

2. Oh you that trouble my Israel, the God of Elijah shall trouble you today, in the name of Jesus.

This message is for those who desire higher level in their lives and ministries. It is for people who are tired of remaining at the bottom rung of the ladder. It is for men, women, young boys and young girls who eye an upward way in their lives.

The purpose of the message is for you to be able to know how to deal with the forces that are retarding your motion in life. The evil forces that are keeping us below where God wants us to be must be accurately dealt with.

When an eternal power is holding someone down, and the one is down-trodden, the enemy goes rejoicing. But, it is not the will of God that the enemy should rejoice over us. If there is any power that keeps you crawling instead of walking or that keeps you walking instead of running, such a power should be frowned at and dealt with as a matter of urgency. Do not joke with such a power. Any power that wants to keep you running when you should be flying should be arrested immediately. You need the deliverance power of the Almighty God to enter into you to deliver you from every negative power that has not allowed you to move ahead in your onward journey.

YOU WERE CREATED TO SUCCEED

God has not created a failure. He designs everyone to succeed. He created everyone with a purpose, for fulfilment in life. The question of whether His eternal purpose is fulfilled for a person's life is a different thing.

It is very important for our enemy to see us attain God's eternal purpose for our lives. Remember that when Jesus was born, the enemy saw His star. Whenever a baby is born, it is possible for men and women, even the people of the underworld to see its destiny. It is equally possible to manipulate God's destiny for a life.

There are people who move about while the enemy has tied down their glorious destiny.

BE GOAL-ORIENTED

The primary step for anyone who desires to be successful is to be goal-oriented. Imagine playing football without a goal post; how would it be known when there is a score? An aeroplane that is flying without a direction will soon crash land. Life would assume no meaning until there is a goal to be pursued.

It is good to have great dreams and visions. It is quite all right to develop big heart for a great exploit in life, ministry or family. But there is a place for goal setting in order to attain God's expectation for each life.

I want to remind you that time flies and does not wait for anyone. Opportunity gained today may be lost tomorrow if not properly handled.

There is nothing that can increase your number of years. You are growing older every day. The earlier you set goals for your life and pursue them, the better for you.

If you fail at setting goals for your life, then you fail elsewhere. If you discover that your life is yet to bring forth God's glory and to become a praise on the earth, then you must set a goal. It is not possible to be a high-flier in life without first becoming a goal-setter.

If you refuse to set a goal then you are already a failure. If setting a goal seems to be a Herculean task for you, then the devil will seek to set goals for you. Believe it or not, the enemy has set goals for many lives and he enforces compliance to the demands of the goals.

This is the more reason several lives today all over the world are having negative success. They succeed only in what the enemy of their souls intends for them. These people are like jellyfish in the hands of their enemy. The devil twists them at will and they show forth the praise of their enemies.

THE TIME IS SHORT

Time is not a friend of anyone. Time is fleeting. They say it is running very fast. It will do our life good if we set goals on time and start to pursue them. Limited time is given to us on earth to prepare for our eternity.

From the day a person is born he starts his journey to the grave. That is why the Bible says that man is like a flower that flourishes in the morning but dies in the evening. The Bible also says our life is like a weaver's shuttle running to and fro. At another place the Bible describes life as the breath at hand. This shows that life is very short indeed. People we meet today will be no more tomorrow. Young men full of life today will soon disappear into oblivion.

The day of one's birthday should be a day of sober reflection because each day draws you closer to the grave. Every celebration of happy birthday is a step towards the day of death. It is a sober reflection that every step a man takes is a step towards his eternal home, either in hell or in heaven. If what we ought to address is not addressed, an eagle-like person may be turned to chicken that cannot fly.

CHARACTER FAILURE

Character failure is the beginning of all failures. It is a major problem that can prevent anyone from soaring high in life. If you would not like to continue to crawl in life, then the issue of character should be well addressed. Many of the problems we encounter in life are as a result of weakness in our character. There are very many people who are wallowing in abject poverty simply because of their character failure. There is no amount of goals you set for yourself that can make you soar high if you have character problems.

Saul failed to deal with his weaknesses which were self-management, self-love and love for praise of men. Although Gehazi was in the school of prophets he failed woefully because of his character. He had the problem of covetousness and lying. Apart from the trial of Abraham's faith, part of the problems he had was lying and the tendency towards cowardice.

The weakness of Moses was anger. This weakness robbed him of access to the Promised Land. Jacob lived a life of defeat until he identified his weakness. He was a cheat, a grabber and a supplanter. He did not only identify his weakness, he cried out unto God in prayer for help. He refused to take "No" for an answer and his name was changed to a prince of God. You too can identify your weaknesses today. Cry unto God for mercy and He will be merciful unto you. He will turn your weakness to strength and you will be able to fulfill His agenda for your life. The weaknesses of David brought curse on him and on his posterity. He had the inability to control his sexual desires. The more you hide away from the truth about the type of life you live, the more the enemy would be promoted in your life. The kingdom of darkness has caged a lot of people in their ovens because of their character.

EAGLE OF MY DESTINY MUST FLY

You must make up your mind that you will not allow your destiny to be marred. Of all things men and women possess, the most precious is their character. Once your character is in shape your destiny is bound to fly. Character is an expedient habit. Habit is what has become part and parcel of you. Your wisdom, talents and gifts can take you to the top, it takes your character to keep you at the top.

Success depends more on character than intelligence or wisdom. Whatsoever you are in the dark when no one is seeing you is your character. If your character is rotten you cannot carve anything out of the rotten wood. If the eagle of your destiny must fly, your character will play a great role.

WHAT IS CHARACTER?

Make a decision and set a goal to develop your character, so that your destiny will be visible to all men. Your character is what you leave behind after you depart from a particular place. Your character is the foundation on which a great edifice of success is built. Your character is like a smoke. It would expose you by and large.

There are many people who will steal if they are sure that they would not be discovered or caught. Your character is your reaction when things are not going the way you wish they would go. There are very many people who are happy when thing are going on normally but when situation changes they show their true colour.

What is character? To answer this question let us consider a fictitious story about Jesus and His disciples.

Jesus and the disciples were going on a very long journey. They were all very weak, worn out and hungry. At a time, Jesus faced the weary disciples and said, "Children, are you hungry?" They answered Him, "Yes, master." He then said, "Please, help me look around, get a stone each and carry it for me." Each of them took a stone and carried it. Some carried a very heavy stone, some carried that of moderate size, while some carried very small stone. Peter picked a very tiny stone that he could easily play with as they moved along. After they had walked some miles, Jesus turned to them again and said,

"Children, are you still hungry." They shouted an overwhelming "Yes, we are." Jesus then commanded their stones to become bread. Those who carried big stones for Jesus had big loaves of bread. Peter who had a tiny stone had a small loaf of bread. Peter soon finished his bread and started begging other disciples for more. He thus learnt his lesson.

A day came again that they were all on a long journey. When they were worn out as usual, Jesus asked them, "Children, are you hungry?" They replied, "Yes, we are." Again He told them, "Locate a stone each and carry it for me." This time, Peter located and carried a very big stone.

As they walked several miles and were very tired, Jesus again asked them, "Are you hungry?" "Yes", they answered. Jesus then said, "If you are hungry then throw away your stones!" When Peter heard "...throw away your stones" he protested, saying: "Master, I have been carrying this stone all along. I thought You will turn it to bread as you did the other day, and that is why I am carrying a big one." Jesus turned to him and asked him, "Who are you carrying the stone for? Is it because of bread or because of me?" The story portrayed what Peter really was. It showed that he obeyed God because of what he could get from Him. His character was shown when things did not really go the way he expected.

Your character is what God knows that you are and not what others think about you. God knows who you are and what you are. Your character is what you stand for. It is your true nature. It is the quality that makes you the kind of person you are. Any flaw in your character or any character failure will keep your eagle down. It will cause your eagle to look like a chicken. Character failure will reduce you to a chicken that cannot fly.

SOURCE OF CHARACTER

The major source of character is heredity. Heredity is characteristic traits that are inborn, which are transferred from parents to their offspring. All human beings are born with certain characteristic traits. These traits might be good or bad. All the bad characteristic traits are inherited and they destroy human beings. When traits are not disciplined and directed they can bring untold failure to anybody. Is your father a liar and are you now lying? It is better you pray to get free from the shackle of demonic traits. Is your father a polygamist and already you are treading his path? You had better resolve this issue before God else your character would double-cross your breakthrough. Many people are into mental and spiritual chaos simply because their characters are obnoxious.

YOU CAN FLY AGAIN

If you want your eagle to fly again, cry unto God to change your character. Identify your evil traits and deal with them. Allow God to put a dirty blow on those evil traits so that you can fly again. Do not be merciful to yourself. Call your evil traits the name they ought to be called. Do not just call them every man's weakness or human insufficiency. Call them the right names. If it is covetousness or pride or stealing call it the right name, so that you can be freed from its shackles. There is freedom for you today if you can cry unto the Lord. When you are sincere about these evil things, the Lord will deliver you right away.

It is possible for us to have a change in character. Looking at the 12 disciples with their characters will tell us that God can change character. The fearful Peter became bold Peter; the revengeful and hot-tempered John was turned to a loving, caring and beloved John.

There is nothing impossible for our God. He can change lives and situations. He can tamper with your character so as to make you become what He wants you to become. That is why I know that you can fly again, for He has not finished with you.

Salvation through the power of the Holy Ghost can bring a great transformation to your way if you allow God the opportunity. When you are.born again, new nature becomes your portion. The Lord will infuse God's nature in you from above. He will bring old things to pass away in your life. This means that salvation and the baptism of the Holy Spirit go a long way in moulding and remoulding our character.

EXAMINE YOURSELF

Do you notice that you are not organised? Has it dawned on you that you are not patient? Do you notice that you are emotionally unstable and that your mood can easily swing? It can be that you lack internal motivation or that you are easily angered.

All these are human traits that can hinder God's purpose for your life. You must ask God to give a dirty blow on these human traits. Examine yourself, take note of those traits that want to stop your upward movement and deal with them in prayer. Your eagle will only fly when you deal decisively with these human traits that are clogs on your wheel of progress.

Do you find it very hard to concentrate on a particular thing? If yes, you may be affected seriously in achieving and maintaining success in life. It will affect your service to God. It will affect your prayer life and it will affect your relationship with both God and men.

If you are a student, lack of concentration will

affect your studies. It will cause you to be jumping from one thing to another without mastering anyone. Examine yourself.

I want you at this point to pray thus: "My father, reveal myself to me, in the name of Jesus."

If you find out that you have a weak will-power, you ought to cry unto the Lord to cause a change in your character.

Are you easily moved to do the wrong thing? Do you live without a principle? Then you need to cry unto God for mercy.

Have you discovered that you lack internal discipline? Examine yourself.

Are you the type of person that likes to please men? Are you always not happy when people are not pleased with you? Watch it, for no men's pleaser will achieve something tangible and substantial.

Are you that kind of person who cannot work hard except he is compelled to do so? Then you ought to cry unto God for a change of character. It is a character disorder for someone not to think of praying except things are out of order.

Do you easily forget things, including your decisions and appointments? It is a character disorder. You need to change. Are you a habitual late comer to meetings or programmes? If yes, then you need a touch of God on your life. Can you be depended on to keep an appointment? Do you like to dominate others in conversation, in decision making and virtually in everything? Do you speak only of yourself in your conversation by always using "I"? If so, you need a change. Examine yourself.

Are you the type that finds it very easy to shed tears? In any little thing you have started weeping and crying.

Are you easily discouraged? Is discouragement your character aberration?

Bow down again at this juncture and pray thus: "My Father, reveal my character to me, in the name of Jesus."

DEAL WITH STRANGERS

These character aberrations are strangers in your life. They are not part of the fruit of the Sprit, neither are they the gifts of the Holy Ghost. They are human weaknesses that prevent the glory of God in a life. They are the servants of the devil that confound and confuse lives and destinies. They must not be allowed to thrive. They must not be allowed to grow. The best bet is to deal with them from the root.

If mercy and compassion have forsaken you in such a way that you are just interested in causing other people to weep and cry, then you ought to deal with such a nature today. Are you very much interested in evil? You need to deal with such a character. Are you hot tempered? Deal with it before it starts to deal with you.

Violent anger is a property of the devil. You must deal with it today. The only anger that God allows is anger against all unrighteousness. When the Bible says that we should be angry and sin not, it means that you should be angry against sin alone. Because there is no way you will be angry without committing sin, except you are angry against sins. Do you have the root of bitterness springing up within you? It is high time you dealt with this evil lest it deals with the foundation of your success.

Are you the type that can pull others down in order to have your way? Do you look down on fellow human beings? If so, deal with these evil traits in you.

Are you the type that does not mind to lobby or use craftiness to secure a position or a seat? If yes, repent and deal with this evil trait.

Are you so proud and stubborn that to apologise to others seems a big task for you? If yes, deal with that Adamic nature in you.

Are you a character assassin? Repent of it and deal with it. If you can deal with these things your life will be glorious and God will depend on you. May you never fail Him that has called you unto Himself. Your life ought to be glorious to such a point that it will give sleepless night to your enemies who want to deal with you. You should make it very difficult for the enemy to manipulate your life.

You cannot make it hard for the enemy when you are very gloomy and sad. Your life would be easily attacked if you are always day-dreaming. If you find it difficult to forgive those who offend you then the enemy would get an easy ride into your life.

Are you sluggish, lazy and indolent? If yes, you will give an express permission to the enemies to enter into your life.

Are you selfish in attitudes, in prayers and in your dealings with people? If yes, you have to cry unto God, who alone is able to save.

Are you always anxious and too eager of how tomorrow would be? This is a character disorder that is a gravedigger and you must be delivered from it.

It is a character disorder if you cannot offer to help another person without demanding for personal gain. If you are doing so, you would be limiting the move of God in your life.

There are also some people who always bite more than they can chew. This is a kind of character

BRINGING DOWN THE POWER OF GOD (47)

disorder that God longs to remove from you for you to have a glamorous future.

WHAT TO DO FOR YOUR DESTINY EAGLE TO FLY AGAIN

1. Study the character of spirit-filled life

There are nine characters of a spirit-filled life, as written in Galatians 5:22-23:

But the fruit of the Spirit is love, joy, peace, longsuffering, gentleness, goodness, faith, Meekness, temperance: against such there is no law.

Study each of them carefully and compare them with what obtains in your life. If you are failing cry for help from above.

2. Make a list of your weaknesses

Making a list of your weaknesses will give you the opportunity of knowing how to deal with them. It will afford you systematic discipline of dealing with these human traits.

firstborn.

The truth of the matter is that the devil hates all the firstborns with perfect hatred and fights them seriously. Immediately the devil knew that there was a good prophecy about Judah the first thing he did was to kill his firstborn mysteriously. Jesus was the only firstborn that looked at the devil eye to eye and dealt with him. It was in the book of Genesis that satan knew that Jesus, the true firstborn, would deal with him. That was why he started to fight every firstborn in the fear of the coming Messiah who was to bruise his head.

If a firstborn is not dedicated to the Lord, the problem in his life will increase. The early Christians understood the principles behind the success or failure of the firstborns.

In the practice of first fruit offering, it is advised that when you get your first salary which is the firstborn of your labour, you should not touch it, or spend it but bring it to God's house. If you do that, then your promotion would be very rapid. Then, special favour would be your portion. I remember that this principle prompted me to give my first salary to God. I took it straight to the pastor, and he prayed for me from the depth of his heart as a result of my obedience to God's instruction. This obedience has seen me through several huddles of life. From that time I received favour anywhere I worked. You may ask, "How would I drop my whole salary to God?" But what would happen if God did not provide the work in the first instance?

The principle of firstborn and first fruit can be traced to the word of God. Even the devil requires first fruits from the people who are serving him. And this is the perversion of God's word.

In some cultures the firstborns are regarded as 'gods'. In some places first fruits are served to the idols. The New Year festival observed in many parts of Nigeria is a perversion of the principle of the first fruit that the Bible commanded.

Test God, by giving out your first fruit, either in cash or in kind, and you will be surprised how He would release blessings on you. If you refuse God the first fruits, the other fruits following may not be quite profiting. The first fruits you give God would release promotion to your life. It would release honour to your life. To those who have spent their first salary, there is hope of redeeming their first fruits to God. You can wait for the beginning of the year and bring the whole first salary of the year to God. Obey God and see what He will do in your life.

A lot of people are ignorant of how Abel automatically received his promotion. Let us looking at this again in Genesis 4:3-4:

And in process of time it came to pass, that Cain brought of the fruit of the ground an offering unto the LORD.

From the above it is clear that Abel brought the first fruit of his flock while Cain brought the remnant to the Lord. That was what prompted the promotion of Abel. Gen. 4:5-7:

But unto Cain and to his offering he had not respect. And Cain was very wroth, and his countenance fell. And the LORD said unto Cain, Why art thou wroth? and why is thy countenance

disorder that God longs to remove from you for you to have a glamorous future.

WHAT TO DO FOR YOUR DESTINY EAGLE TO FLY AGAIN

1. Study the character of spirit-filled life

There are nine characters of a spirit-filled life, as written in Galatians 5:22-23:

But the fruit of the Spirit is love, joy, peace, longsuffering, gentleness, goodness, faith, Meekness, temperance: against such there is no law.

Study each of them carefully and compare them with what obtains in your life. If you are failing cry for help from above.

2. Make a list of your weaknesses

Making a list of your weaknesses will give you the opportunity of knowing how to deal with them. It will afford you systematic discipline of dealing with these human traits.

3. See these weaknesses as sins

Do not point accusing fingers to anyone. Do not call these traits beautiful names that would not show their evil gravity. Call them sins. Call them evils. Call them iniquities or wickedness so that you can deal with them in the best possible way.

4. Ask for victory over these traits

To be freed from them, be involved in specific targeted prayers against them.

5. Be filled with the Holy Ghost

There are things the Holy Ghost wants to reveal to you. Blessed are you if you think on these things and make your way right before Him.

CHAPTER THREE

THE LOST SECRET
OF THE CHURCH

Raise your right hand and pray thus: "Every conspiracy in the heavenlies against my destiny, scatter, in the name of Jesus."

The understanding of church history will reveal that few years after the crucifixion of our Lord Jesus Christ, His disciples spread Christianity all over the then known world.

In spite of the persecution from Emperor Nero and the aggression of the Roman Empire, half of the people of the empire became secret disciples of Christ.

Although they were not as educated as many of us are today, these disciples turned the whole world upside down. It then appears that there are certain things regarding the kingdom that those disciples knew which we do not know. They walked in a realm that the present-day crops of believers are ignorant of. They attained this feat with little or no communication technology that we have today. They did not even have the printed Bibles in their hands.

In spite of the assistance the modern day

Christians have from the radio, the television, the print media, books, travelling and education, they have accomplished far less than what the apostles did within few years. Could it be that the first church knew certain secrets which the present-day believers do not know?

A close examination of their messages show that we are preaching the same messages they preached, but the impact they made was far greater than the impact being made by the modern day church.

THE LOST SECRETS OF PRESENT-DAY CHRISTIANITY

When a thing is referred to as "secret", it means such a thing is not open to everybody. It means it is not everybody that has access to such a thing. All people do not have knowledge of a thing called "secret". Someone can look at a secret thing that makes things work without having knowledge of such a thing. You may meet an angel or the personality of the Holy Spirit without taking cognisance of him.

Men can be very ignorant of spiritual things. What are the secrets that the apostles concentrated upon?

1. *Holy Spirit was deeply emphasised in their ministry*

The teaching of the apostles was deeply rooted in the work of the Holy Spirit more than in human teaching. The will of the Lord is that you should be filled with the Holy Spirit, so that everything you do will be done under the auspices of the Holy Spirit.

The book of the Acts says that the Holy Spirit came upon Peter and he opened his mouth and started preaching and teaching by His power. He was not using his human reasoning and wisdom. If the church of God can do the same today, it will be the beginning of great revival and the outbreak of God's power in our midst. Paul too was filled with the Holy Ghost and he spoke with His power.

Many of our speech, teaching and preaching carry no fire because of lack of the infilling of the Holy Spirit.

Lack of power, grace and glory in the church today

is due to the dilution of the teaching of the Holy Spirit with human theology.

The ignorance of the modern-day Christianity is so pronounced to the level that anyone who is truly filled with the Holy Spirit is accused of operating under demonic influence.

2. Emphasis on churches at home rather than the church building

The house fellowship structure of the apostles of those days was very strong. Many Christians today are not bothered about house fellowship because they do not know it is the secret of church growth. Some believe that they are greater and higher than the house fellowship. But house fellowship is God's way of spreading His fire across the land.

It is the quickest way of possessing our environment for God. If the church is persecuted, the only thing that would be left is for her to meet at house fellowship level.

3. *The Apostles emphasised yoke-breaking by the anointing*

4. *They regarded themselves as a single unit*

They were bounded together in love. There was no division or schism among them. That was why God was able to bless them mightily.

5. *They prayed powerful prayers*

The Bible says that when the Apostles gathered together the place they were praying was shaken. They prayed powerful prayers.

6. *The Lord is demanding both first born and the first fruits*

This is another secret that the apostles had. Look at Exodus 22:29:

Thou shalt not delay to offer the first of thy ripe fruits, and of thy liquors: the firstborn of thy sons shalt thou give unto me.

Here the Lord is asking for the first born and the first fruits, respectively.

Why is God asking for the first born and the first

fruits? Let us get the answer from Genesis 49:3:

Reuben, thou art my firstborn, my might, and the beginning of my strength, the excellency of dignity, and the excellency of power:

This statement was made by Jacob when he said his popular prayer for his children, when he was about to die. Consider the implication of firstborn in that verse: "my might, beginning of my strength, excellency of dignity and excellency of power."

There are many firstborns who are not finding their feet. There are many firstborns whose lifestyles are like those of the last born. God Himself adopted Israel as His firstborn.

God's first born (Israel) were once in Egypt. God demanded that His firstborn should be released and Pharaoh refused. But Pharaoh had no option but to release them by the time God dealt with all the firstborn in Egypt.

The lesson drawn from the issue of firstborn is that whatsoever is first belongs to God because God is the first.

There would always be trouble for any firstborn dedicated to any other thing besides God. Once a firstborn is not dedicated to God there is a serious battle for him. Jesus is also God's firstborn. God needs the firstborn.

Just as God is much interested in the firstborn of man, He is also much interested in the firstborns of every other thing.

There are firstborns in the Bible who were not successful.

Take Cain and Abel for example. Cain failed but Abel succeeded.

There were Ishmael and Isaac. Isaac was chosen but Ishmael was not.

Another were Esau and Jacob. Esau was the firstborn but he was not chosen.

Another example was Reuben and Joseph. Reuben was the firstborn but he was not chosen.

There were Manasseh and Ephraim. Manasseh was the firstborn but he was not chosen.

There were Aaron and Moses. Aaron the elder was not chosen but Moses.

There were the brothers of David in the Bible. Eliab was the oldest but He was not chosen. David was chosen.

A careful student of the Bible would realise that it is silent about the mother of David. He might have been born by another mother and not the mother of the rest of his brethren. All his brothers were old enough to give birth to him. When Jesse was asked to bring all his sons, he did not count David as a person to be reckoned with as a likely king; he was not regarded because he was quite small. Yet, Eliab failed and David succeeded.

There was another man called Adonijah, the first child of David. He was not chosen as the king but Solomon. Almost all the first borns from Genesis to Malachi ended up being failures. It looks difficult to find any firstborn who really pleased God.

Remember that Noah was not the firstborn. Joseph was not the firstborn and David was not the firstborn.

The truth of the matter is that the devil hates all the firstborns with perfect hatred and fights them seriously. Immediately the devil knew that there was a good prophecy about Judah the first thing he did was to kill his firstborn mysteriously. Jesus was the only firstborn that looked at the devil eye to eye and dealt with him. It was in the book of Genesis that satan knew that Jesus, the true firstborn, would deal with him. That was why he started to fight every firstborn in the fear of the coming Messiah who was to bruise his head.

If a firstborn is not dedicated to the Lord, the problem in his life will increase. The early Christians understood the principles behind the success or failure of the firstborns.

In the practice of first fruit offering, it is advised that when you get your first salary which is the firstborn of your labour, you should not touch it, or spend it but bring it to God's house. If you do that, then your promotion would be very rapid. Then, special favour would be your portion. I remember that this principle prompted me to give my first salary to God. I took it straight to the pastor, and he prayed for me from the depth of his heart as a result of my obedience to God's instruction. This obedience has seen me through several huddles of life. From that time I received favour anywhere I worked. You may ask, "How would I drop my whole salary to God?" But what would happen if God did not provide the work in the first instance?

The principle of firstborn and first fruit can be traced to the word of God. Even the devil requires first fruits from the people who are serving him. And this is the perversion of God's word.

In some cultures the firstborns are regarded as 'gods'. In some places first fruits are served to the idols. The New Year festival observed in many parts of Nigeria is a perversion of the principle of the first fruit that the Bible commanded.

Test God, by giving out your first fruit, either in cash or in kind, and you will be surprised how He would release blessings on you. If you refuse God the first fruits, the other fruits following may not be quite profiting. The first fruits you give God would release promotion to your life. It would release honour to your life. To those who have spent their first salary, there is hope of redeeming their first fruits to God. You can wait for the beginning of the year and bring the whole first salary of the year to God. Obey God and see what He will do in your life.

A lot of people are ignorant of how Abel automatically received his promotion. Let us looking at this again in Genesis 4:3-4:

And in process of time it came to pass, that Cain brought of the fruit of the ground an offering unto the LORD.

From the above it is clear that Abel brought the first fruit of his flock while Cain brought the remnant to the Lord. That was what prompted the promotion of Abel. Gen. 4:5-7:

But unto Cain and to his offering he had not respect. And Cain was very wroth, and his countenance fell. And the LORD said unto Cain, Why art thou wroth? and why is thy countenance

fallen? If thou doest well, shalt thou not be accepted? and if thou doest not well, sin lieth at the door. And unto thee shall be his desire, and thou shalt rule over him.

God told Cain that he cold still give his first fruits by waiting for the next opportunity the following year. But instead of waiting he became envious of the promotion of his brother and therefore eliminated him.

Your unremitted tithes will make your income accessible to the spiritual robbers. Your tithes would keep the windows of heaven open for you permanently and your first fruit offering would determine your promotion. It would determine your increase and growth. Your first fruit offering would determine the rate of your enlargement. It is very clear that God wants the firstborns as well as the first fruits. The principles were handed over to the patriarchs and they practised them.

There are bad records about many firstborn in the Bible. If you are a firstborn, you need deliverance and redemption. God is very serious about firstborns because they are the first fruits that are to be offered unto Him. The issue raised is not just the baby dedication. Many dedicated in the church when they were babies were later executed at the Bar beach.

The firstborn offering implies offering the firstborn child unto God. Looking at the people with deliverance problems will prove to us that firstborns seem to have more deliverance problem than the rest. Only very few firstborns escape the tormenting hands of the devil.

WHY FIRSTBORNS ARE ALWAYS IN TROUBLE

1. *When someone who was bitten by a serpent before sees a worm, he would be scared, thinking that it is a serpent.* Since the devil was defeated by Jesus, who is the firstborn of God, the devil has hated the firstborns of all mankind. He has always seen the firstborn as a terror to him and his kingdom. He hates the firstborns whether they are serving

God or not.

2.   *Devil hates the firstborn because God says that they belong to Him.* That is why they become regular satanic targets.

3.   *The firstborns are the only children with commandments attached to them.*

4.   *The firstborns are always victims of parental inexperience and ignorance.* Most often they are used in teaching practice for their parental roles.

5.   *The firstborns are regarded as heirs to the father's seat.*

6.   *The firstborns are the beasts of burden for the whole family.* They set their backs to carry other children.

7.   *Sometimes the firstborns are used as spiritual torchlight.* They face all the initial dangers and other children that follow them start to enjoy themselves at the beam of their light. That is the reason the Bible says that if there are six children in a family their inheritance should be shared into seven

parts and two of the parts should be given to the firstborn.

The truth is this, when any firstborn is redeemed, he can get his double portion back. Let us read Proverb 3:9-10:

When your fathers tempted me, proved me, and saw my works forty years. Wherefore I was grieved with that generation, and said, They do alway err in their heart; and they have not known my ways.

Your first fruit will give you access to progress and promotion in life.

THE BLESSINGS FOR THE OBEDIENT

There are always blessings attached to people who obey God in their first fruit offering. As you practise this principle, wonderful favours and powerful promotions will come your way. These are secrets that most people do not practise. That is why they remain the same all their years. People refuse this kind of message sometimes out of ignorance or out of unbelief and sometimes out of being stingy towards God.

Everybody, including students and apprentices, can pay their first fruit unto God, and then wait to see what He will do. The first income that comes to your hands belongs to the Lord. If you refuse to obey God, He misses nothing but you are depriving yourself of His blessings. If you determine not to pay your tithe, for example, God is not moved, but you are the one who has stopped His blessings from flowing in your life. Spiritual robbers can then come to deal with you.

I remember my undergraduate years when we were about to have an examination. I had two note books on Organic Chemistry. They were stolen and I was left with virtually nothing to read, except the concluding part of our lessons which was about one quarter of the whole content of the notes on Organic Chemistry.

I cried unto God and He told me, "Son, your first fruit offering will speak for you."

When I got to the study room, the concluding note

book took me just two hours to read. Having nothing further to read I slept off waiting for whatever would happen the next day of the examination.

When the examination questions were brought the next day, there was not a single question from the note books that were stolen. All questions were drawn from the concluding note which I read for two hours. I then began to feel sorry for the thief who would have read the stolen note books throughout the night. God favoured me and saw me through on the basis of my first fruit offering.

If the situation of first fruit is not attended to on time, it then become what was found in Isa. 14:30:

And the firstborn of the poor shall feed, and the needy shall lie down in safety: and I will kill thy root with famine, and he shall slay thy remnant.

When someone is the firstborn of the poor, or the most miserable of the poor, he has harder work to do. There is always a need for family deliverance for all the firstborns so that their lives can be as God wants them to be.

PRAYER POINTS

1. You power of the oppressor, let my family go, in the name of Jesus.

2. Thou power of frustration, your time is up, therefore die, in the name of Jesus.

3. Every power feeding on my victory, die, in the name of Jesus.

4. Every arrow of untimely death, backfire, in the name of Jesus.

5. Every foundational wickedness in my father's house, your time is up, die, in the name of Jesus.

6. Yokes of hardship, yokes of poverty, yokes of demotion, break, in the name of Jesus.

7. Progress arresters, be arrested, in the name of Jesus.

8. Every curse that is affecting my breakthrough, by the power in the blood of Jesus, die, in the name of Jesus.

Other Publications by Dr. D. K. Olukoya

Other Publications by Dr. D. K. Olukoya

Other Publications by Dr. D. K. Olukoya

Other Publications by Dr. D. K. Olukoya

ANNUAL 70 DAYS PRAYER AND FASTING PUBLICATIONS

ABOUT THE *Book*

Bringing Down The Power of God is a dynamic exposition of the power of God which is able to save to the uttermost. Using familiar Bible passages, the author, with an uncommon desterity portrays timeless Biblical principles on what it takes to obtain and retain spiritual power.

The approach is unique, the prayer points are acidic while the presentation of each chapter makes the book invaluable companion to this who are hungry for the undiluted power of God.

This book will enable you to say goodbye to powerlessness.

ABOUT THE *Author*

Dr. D. K. Olukoya is the General Overseer of the Mountain of Fire and Miracles Ministries and The Battle Cry Christian Ministries.

The Mountain of Fire and Miracles Ministries' Headquarters is the largest single christian congregation in Africa with attendance of over 120,000 in single meetings.

MFM is a full gospel ministry devoted to the revival of Apostolic signs, Holy Ghost Fireworks, miracles and the unlimited demonstration of the power of God to deliver to the uttermost. Absolute holiness within and without as spiritual insecticide and pre-requisite for heaven is openly taught. MFM is a do-it-yourself Gospel Ministry, where your hands are trained to wage war and your fingers to do battle.

Dr. Olukoya holds a first class honours degree in Micro-biology from the University of Lagos and a PhD in Molecular Genetics from the University of Reading, United Kingdom. As a researcher, he has over seventy scientific publications to his credit.

Anointed by God, Dr. Olukoya is a prophet, evangelist, teacher and preacher of the Word. His life and that of his wife, Shade and their son, Elijah Toluwani are living proofs that all power belongs to God.

ISBN 978-978-49178-0-3

978-978-49178-0-3

www.ingramcontent.com/pod-product-compliance
Lightning Source LLC
LaVergne TN
LVHW051155080426
835508LV00021B/2637